THIS COLORING BELONG TO :

I0789053

COLOR THE FLOWER

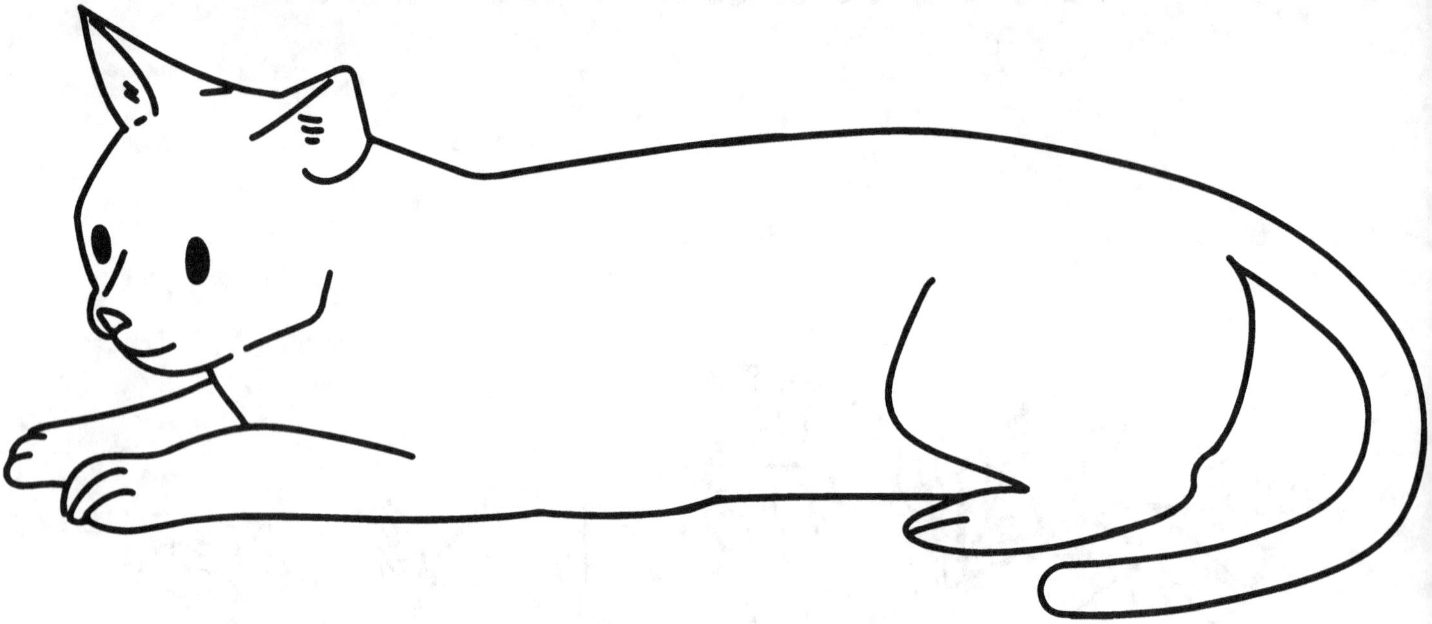

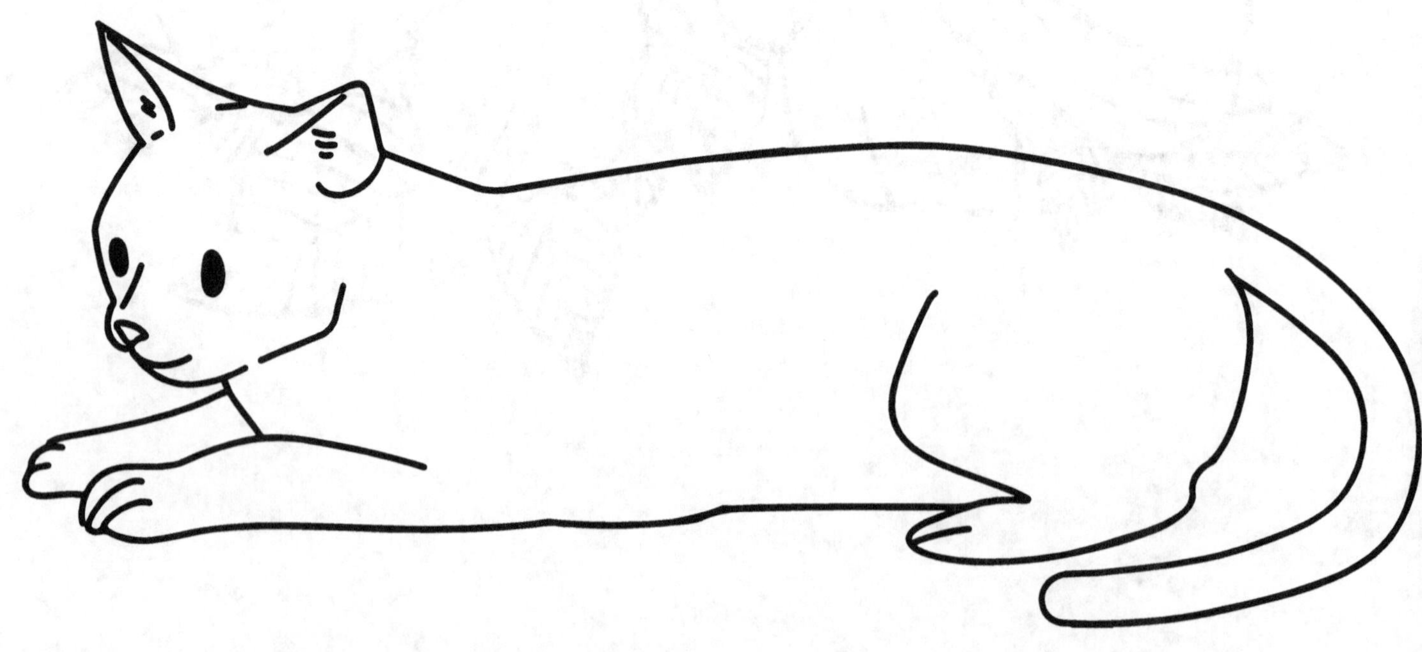

COLOR THE FLOWER

COLOR THE FLOWER

COLOR THE FLOWER

COLOR THE FLOWER

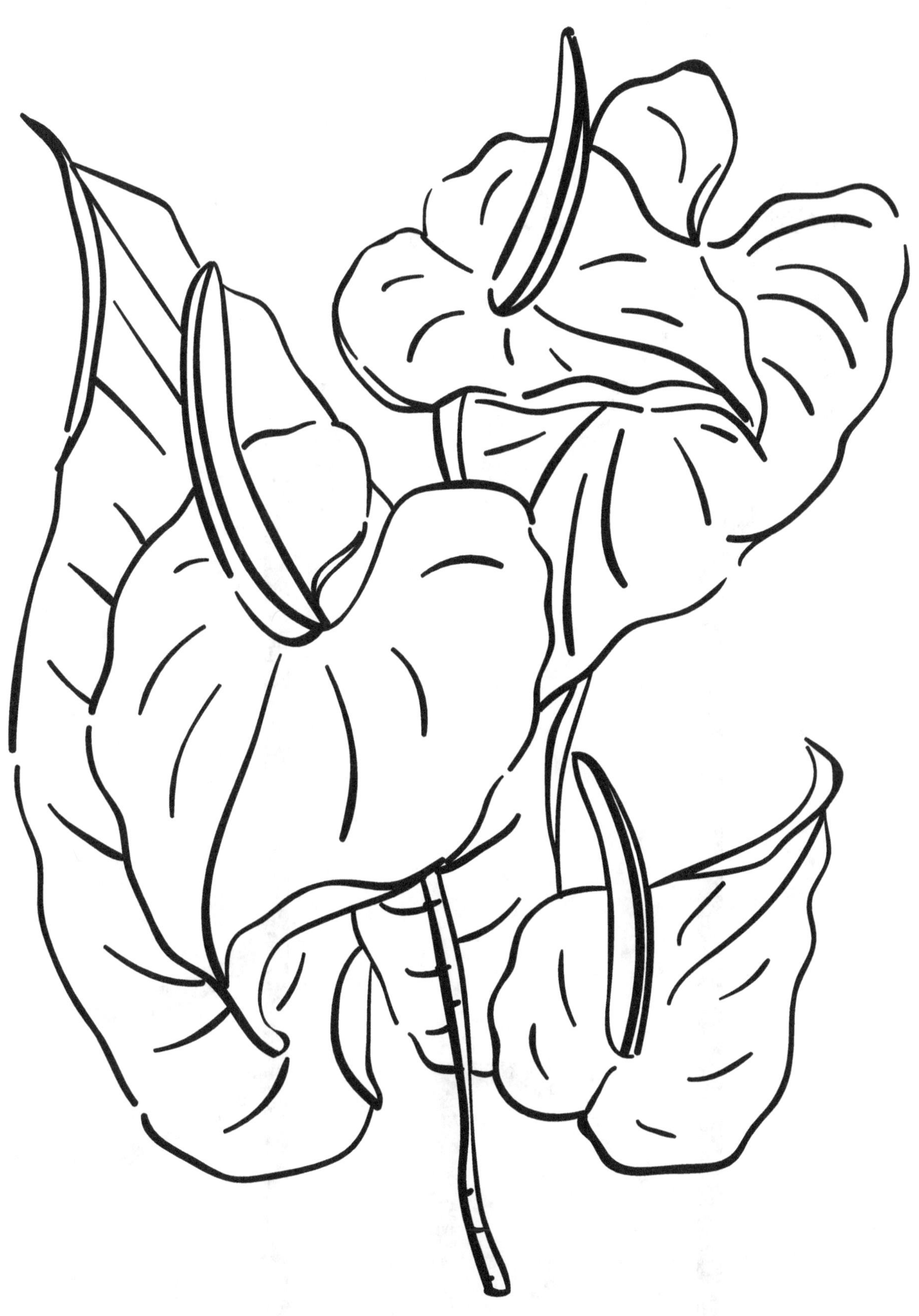

COLOR THE FLOWER

COLOR THE FLOWER

COLOR THE FLOWER

COLOR THE FLOWER

COLOR THE FLOWER

COLOR THE FLOWER

COLOR THE FLOWER

COLOR THE FLOWER

COLOR THE FLOWER

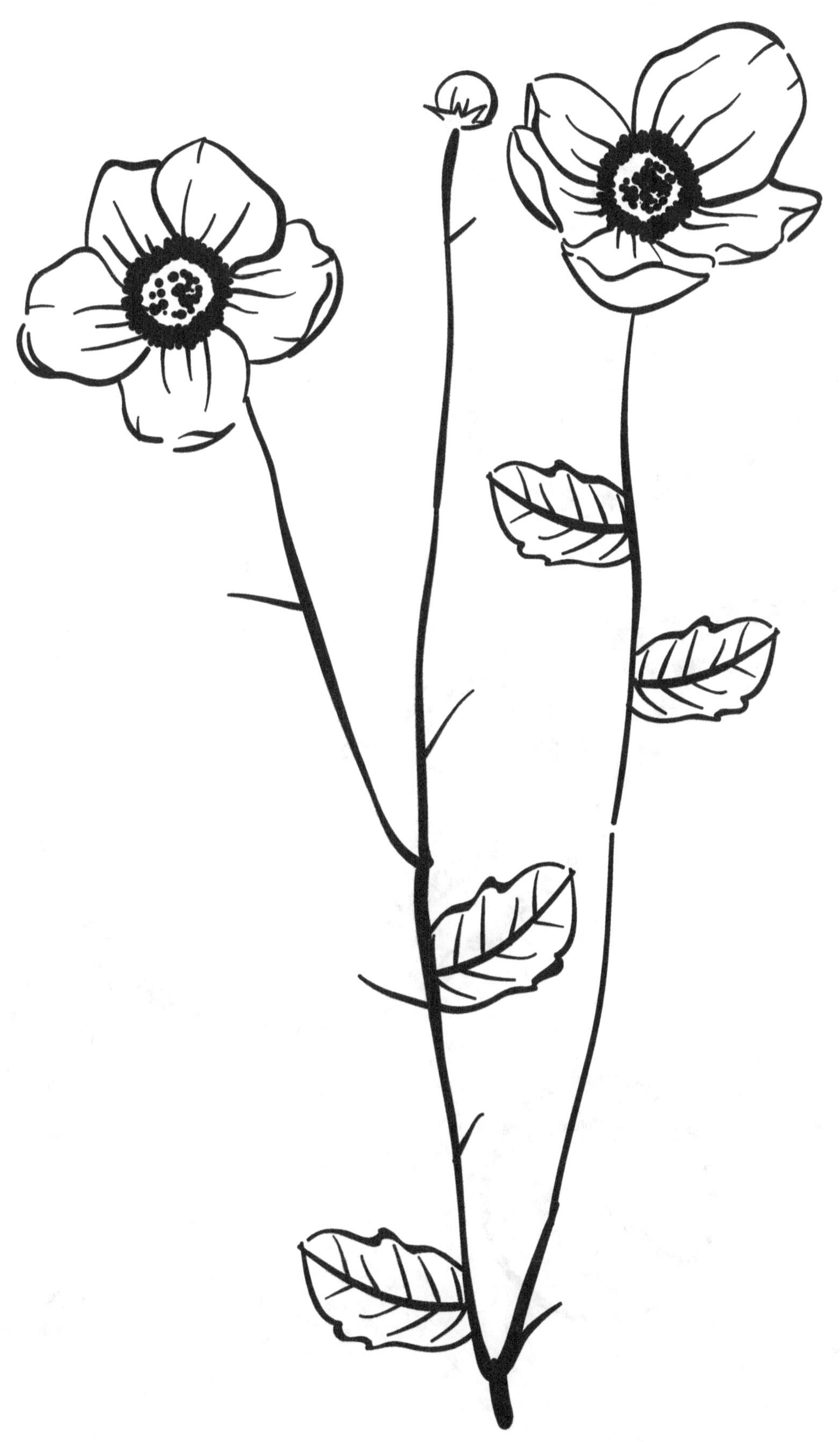

COLOR THE FLOWER

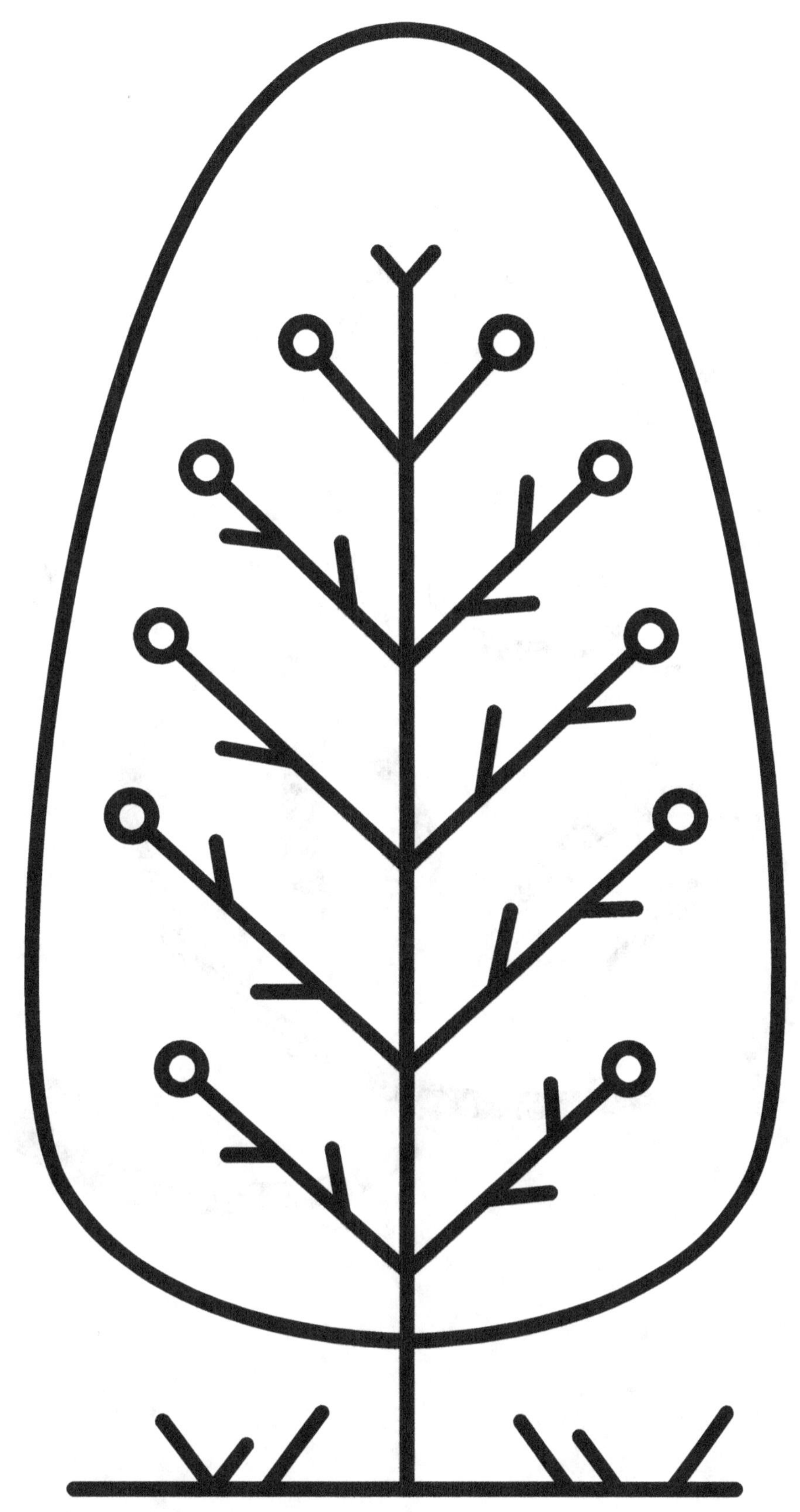